Tuli Rose

# Everyone Needs a Digital Asset and a Robotic Vacuum

# Peek Inside

# Assets, Time, Transformation

Hey there, and a warm welcome to "Everyone Needs a Digital Asset and a Robotic Vacuum" I'm Tuli Rose, and I'm thrilled you're joining me on this journey. If you've ever found yourself caught in the relentless cycle of the 9-17 grind, dreaming of a life where your time truly belongs to you, then, my friend, you're in the right place.

This book is born out of a simple yet profound realization: in our digitally-driven era, creating digital assets isn't just a smart move; it's essential. And while we're at it, why not embrace the marvels of modern technology to make our daily lives a tad easier? Enter the robotic vacuum – a symbol of the practical, time-saving tools that can transform our lives.

Through these pages, we'll dive deep into the 'how' and 'why' of digital assets, breaking down the barriers that might have held you back. We'll explore the incredible potential of passive income, the beauty of financial freedom, and yes, how a robotic vacuum can be the unlikely hero in your quest for a better quality of life.

I promise to keep things light, engaging, and above all, real. We'll share laughs, maybe shed a tear (of joy, I hope!), and most importantly, we'll navigate this journey together. By the end, my goal is for you to see the endless possibilities that digital assets and a bit of automation can bring into your life.

So, grab your favorite beverage, find a comfy spot, and let's turn the page on a new chapter of your life. It's time to unlock the potential within you and embrace the change that's just waiting to unfold.

Welcome aboard. Let's make some magic happen.

# The Value of Time

Time. It's that elusive, ever-ticking companion that seems to slip through our fingers like grains of sand. We all get the same 24 hours in a day, yet how often do we find ourselves wishing for just a little more? "If only I had more time," we lament, as yet another day closes, and we're left wondering where it all went.

But here's the thing about time – it's not about having more of it; it's about making the most of what we've got. It's about those quiet moments in the early morning when the world is still asleep, and you're up, sipping your coffee, plotting your next big move. It's about the stolen moments late at night, under the soft glow of a desk lamp, as you tap away at your keyboard, bringing your dreams to life, one word at a time.

The realization hit me like a ton of bricks one ordinary Tuesday. There I was, buried under a mountain of work, the clock mocking me with its relentless ticking. It dawned on me that I was trading my most valuable asset for something that, in the grand scheme of things, held far less value. I was trading my time for money, yes, but at what cost? My creativity? My freedom? My peace of mind?

It's a common trap we fall into, measuring our worth by how busy we are, equating a packed schedule with productivity, with success. But true success, I've come to learn, isn't about how much you can cram into your day; it's about making space for the things that truly matter. It's about creating, not consuming; it's about living, not just existing.

So, I made a pact with myself. No longer would I be a slave to the clock, to the endless cycle of work, eat, sleep, repeat. I decided to reclaim my time, to use it as a canvas for my creativity, as a foundation for building a life that brings me joy, fulfillment, and yes, even financial freedom.

And that's where digital assets come into play. The beauty of creating something digital is that you do it once, and it has the potential to pay dividends for years to come. It's like planting a seed and watching it grow, each sale, each download, a testament to the timeless value of what you've created.

But let's not get ahead of ourselves. Creating digital assets, be it a book, a course, or a piece of art, is not about quick wins or easy money. It's about investing your time wisely, about pouring your heart and soul into something that matters, something that has the potential to change not just your life, but the lives of others.

As I embarked on this journey, I learned to see time not as my enemy, but as my ally. With each passing day, I became more intentional about how I spent my hours, more discerning about the projects I took on, and more passionate about the work I put out into the world.

And you know what? It changed everything. My relationship with time, with work, with myself. I found freedom in the discipline of creation, joy in the act of sharing my knowledge, and a deep, abiding satisfaction in knowing that, in my own small way, I was making a difference.

So, as you turn the pages of this book, as you ponder the possibilities that lie ahead, remember this: time is the most precious commodity we have. Spend it wisely, invest it in things that matter, and watch as your life transforms in ways you never thought possible.

# The Revelation of Digital Assets

It hit me out of nowhere, this idea of digital assets. There I was, aimlessly scrolling through Etsy, when I stumbled upon a digital guide for crafting with avocado pits. Yes, you read that right. Avocado pits. And it was selling like hotcakes. That's when the gears started turning, and a light bulb went off in my head. If someone could turn avocado pits into gold, what was stopping me – or anyone, for that matter – from creating something out of our own unique experiences and knowledge?

Let me back up a bit and clarify what I mean by "digital assets." In the simplest terms, a digital asset is anything digital that you can create once and sell multiple times. It could be an eBook, a course, a piece of music, a photograph, or even a crafting guide for using avocado pits. The beauty of digital assets lies in their scalability. You put in the work once, and it has the potential to generate income repeatedly, without the need for constant hands-on effort.

The revelation was profound. We live in an era where information is currency, and expertise, no matter how niche or seemingly trivial, has value. Each one of us possesses a unique set of skills, experiences, and perspectives that can offer something valuable to the world. And the best part? There's a market for almost everything under the sun.

Take, for example, a viral interview I saw with a six-year-old who wrote a series of books. When asked why she chose to write, she said it was because she wanted to buy an apartment. Why books, you might ask? Because, in her words, "it's something you do once and sell many times". That's the power of digital assets. They break down barriers, democratize entrepreneurship, and open up a world of possibilities for anyone with a story to tell, a skill to share, or an idea to spread.

Now, you might be thinking, "But I'm not an expert in anything." To that, I say, think again. Expertise isn't just about holding degrees or having years of experience. It's about passion, curiosity, and the willingness to share what you know. Whether you're a hobbyist baker with a killer cookie recipe, a weekend gardener with tips for growing the perfect tomato, or even someone who's navigated personal challenges and come out stronger on the other side, you have something valuable to offer.

Creating digital assets is also an empowering act. It's about taking control of your time, your income, and your creative expression. It's about building something that can not only boost your financial situation but also contribute to your sense of purpose and self-worth. And let's not forget the impact you can have on others. Your knowledge, shared, has the power to inform, inspire, and transform lives.

The journey to creating digital assets is not without its challenges. It requires time, effort, and a willingness to learn and adapt. But the rewards, both tangible and intangible, are immeasurable. It's about more than just making money; it's about making a difference, leaving a legacy, and creating something that, long after you've moved on to your next project, continues to educate, entertain, and enlighten.

So, as we delve deeper into the world of digital assets, remember this: the only limits to what you can achieve are those you place on yourself. With the right mindset, a dash of creativity, and a willingness to put yourself out there, the possibilities are endless. Let's embark on this journey together, exploring the untapped potential within each of us and turning our knowledge and passions into digital treasures that can enrich not just our lives, but the lives of others around the globe.

# Exploring the Landscape of Digital Assets

In the digital realm, the possibilities for creating assets that can generate passive income are vast and varied. This chapter aims to demystify the world of digital assets by presenting a straightforward list of options available to creators, entrepreneurs, and hobbyists alike. Each entry includes a brief explanation and practical ideas to help you get started. The focus is on accessible, doable projects that don't require complex technical skills or significant upfront investment.

- **E-Books**: Compile your expertise or creative writing into an e-book. Structure it with a clear introduction, detailed chapters on specific topics, and a conclusion. Include visuals or worksheets to add value.

- **Online Courses**: Share your knowledge through video or text-based courses. Break down the course into modules covering different aspects of the subject, with quizzes to test understanding.

- **Printables**: Create downloadable printables, such as planners, checklists, or decorative items. Design them in a PDF format with sections for daily, weekly, or monthly planning, specific projects, or themed decorations.

- **Stock Photography**: Offer collections of your photographs for sale. Organize them by themes such as nature, urban landscapes, or lifestyle to make them more searchable for potential buyers.

- **Digital Art**: Sell your artwork online. You can create digital paintings, illustrations, or graphic designs and sell them as downloadable files or through print-on-demand services.

- **Music and Sound Effects**: Produce and sell your music tracks, beats, or sound effects. Package them based on genres or use cases, like background music for videos, meditation, or podcasts.

- **Templates and Themes**: Develop templates for websites, presentations, or social media. Offer a variety of styles and layouts catering to different industries or personal preferences.

- **Mobile Apps**: If you have a simple app idea, consider

developing it. Focus on solving a specific problem or entertaining, with a user-friendly design and intuitive functionality.

- **Podcasts**: Start a podcast on a topic you're passionate about. You can monetize through sponsorships, memberships, or selling bonus content.

- **Digital Workshops and Webinars**: Host live or pre-recorded sessions on topics you specialize in. Include interactive elements like Q&A sessions, workbooks, and actionable takeaways.

- **Subscription Services**: Create a membership platform offering exclusive content, like advanced tutorials, insider tips, or specialized resources.

- **Digital Patterns and Crafts**: For those into crafts, design sewing, knitting, or woodworking patterns. Provide clear instructions, diagrams, and necessary templates for each project.

- **Software and Tools**: Develop simple tools or software that address specific needs. Focus on ease of use and how it solves problems for your target audience.

- **E-Newsletters**: Curate and send out newsletters on niche topics. Monetize through ads, sponsorships, or exclusive content for subscribers.

- **Guides and Manuals**: Write in-depth guides or how-to manuals on specific subjects. Structure them with step-by-step instructions, FAQs, and troubleshooting tips.

By focusing on these digital assets, you can explore various avenues to generate income based on your skills, interests, and the resources available to you. The key is to start small, experiment, and gradually build your digital portfolio.

# The Universe of Digital Assets

Diving into the universe of digital assets is like stepping into a vast, ever-expanding galaxy. Each star represents a different kind of digital asset, shining brightly with potential. From eBooks to online courses, from stock photography to digital templates, the variety is staggering, and the opportunities are boundless.

Let's start with eBooks, a cornerstone of the digital asset world. Writing an eBook can seem like a daunting task, but remember the story of the six-year-old author? If she can do it, so can you. eBooks can cover any topic under the sun. Passionate about cooking? Write a recipe book. Fascinated by mindfulness? Pen down your practices and tips. The key is to find a niche that resonates with you and to which you can contribute authentically.

Next up, online courses. The thirst for knowledge in our digital age is unquenchable, making educational content incredibly valuable. You don't need a teaching degree to create a course. What you need is expertise or passion for a subject and a desire to share it. Platforms like Udemy, Coursera, and Teachable have democratized education, allowing anyone to teach anything. Whether it's coding, painting, or even avocado pit crafting, there's an audience waiting to learn from you.

But let's not stop there. The universe of digital assets extends beyond words and courses. Photography enthusiasts can sell their photos on stock websites like Shutterstock or create preset filters for Instagram. Graphic designers can sell templates for websites, resumes, or social media posts. Musicians can produce beats or soundtracks. The list goes on.

The creation of digital assets also extends to software and apps. If you have a knack for coding, developing a useful app or a game can be a goldmine. Even simple utility apps, like a unit converter or a daily planner, can provide significant value to someone's day-to-day life.

One of the most fascinating aspects of digital assets is their scalability. Create once, sell forever. Your eBook, once written, can be sold to an unlimited number of readers without any additional effort on your part. Your online course can educate thousands, even while you sleep. This passive income stream allows you to "earn while you live," giving you the financial freedom to explore other passions or simply enjoy life.

But here's the thing about the universe of digital assets: it's constantly evolving. New platforms, new formats, and new opportunities emerge all the time. Staying curious and open to learning is crucial. The digital asset you create today might open doors to opportunities you never imagined tomorrow.

Creating digital assets is not just about generating income; it's about leveraging your unique insights, skills, and passions to contribute something of value to the world. It's about leaving a digital footprint that can inspire, educate, and entertain long after you've moved on to your next project.

As we journey through this vast universe together, remember that every one of us has something to offer. The digital age has democratized the creation and distribution of knowledge, making it possible for anyone to share their light with the world. So, what's your digital asset going to be? Let's explore, create, and shine together.

# Beyond Profession - Your Hobbies as Assets

In the woven fabric of our lives, our professions often take the spotlight, while our hobbies wait patiently in the wings, their potential untapped, simmering beneath the surface. But what if I told you that these hobbies, these passions pursued in the quiet corners of our evenings and weekends, hold the key to unlocking a treasure trove of digital assets? That's right — your hobbies are not just pastimes; they're potential gold mines.

Let's take a moment to shift our perspective. Imagine a world where your weekend gardening, your nightly guitar strumming, or your fascination with vintage comic books isn't just a means to unwind but a pathway to creating something valuable, something shareable, something that can enrich both your life and the lives of others. This chapter is about seeing beyond the daily grind of your profession and recognizing the wealth of opportunity lying dormant in your hobbies.

Consider the gardener whose hands are as comfortable in the soil as they are on a keyboard, chronicling the journey of seed to bloom. A blog, an eBook, or even a series of how-to videos on sustainable gardening practices can inspire a greener thumb in others and contribute to a more sustainable world. Each post, page, or video is a digital asset, blooming with the potential for growth and income.

Or the amateur guitarist, whose evenings are spent coaxing melodies from strings. Those chord progressions, those riffs born from hours of practice and passion, can be transformed into an online course, teaching others to find their musical voice. Imagine a digital asset that not only earns income but also brings the joy of music into someone else's life.

And let's not forget the comic book enthusiast, whose love for storytelling through panels and speech bubbles transcends mere collection. Crafting a guide to the golden age of comics, or creating original artwork inspired by classic heroes, can turn a personal hobby into a shared digital asset. Your passion for the medium becomes a beacon for fellow enthusiasts and newcomers alike, illuminating the artistry and history of comic books.

The beauty of transforming hobbies into digital assets lies in the authenticity and joy infused in every creation. When you create from a place of passion, your work resonates with a unique voice, a genuine enthusiasm that is both infectious and inspiring. These creations are not just assets; they're extensions of yourself, shared with the world.

But beyond the joy and the potential for income, turning hobbies into digital assets offers something even more valuable: a reminder that our lives are rich with potential, that every passion pursued, every hobby nurtured, is a stepping stone towards a life less ordinary. It's a call to break free from the notion that our professions define us and to embrace the multitude of facets that make up our identities.

As we journey through the process of transforming hobbies into digital assets, remember that the path is as rewarding as the destination. The act of creating, of sharing your passions with the world, is a testament to the idea that everyone has something of value to offer. So, dust off your gardening tools, tune your guitar, and flip through your comic collection with a new lens. The world is waiting for what you have to share.

In this chapter, we've only scratched the surface of the possibilities that lie in your hobbies. As you close this section and ponder the potential within your passions, remember that the journey from hobbyist to creator of digital assets is not just about the income you might earn but about the fulfillment, growth, and connections you'll experience along the way. Your hobbies are not just hobbies; they're the keys to new worlds waiting to be explored.

# Inspired to Create

After a quick dive into Google and Etsy, I've pulled together a sweet summary of assets that folks are actually making money from — just for you. This chapter is all about showing you that no matter what you're into — be it making things neater with planners or getting smart with budgeting — you've got something valuable to share. We've got a bunch of ideas here to get those wheels turning in your head. It's all about making your passion or day-job skills work for you in the digital world. So, let's dive in and see what clicks for you!

- **Customizable Planners** - $5 to $20: Planners for various needs, including daily, weekly, or monthly organization.

- **Printable Wall Art** - $3 to $15: Artwork that customers can print at home for their personal use.

- **Sewing Patterns** - $4 to $10: Patterns for clothing, accessories, or home decor items.

- **Knitting and Crochet Patterns** - $3 to $8: Patterns for creating knit or crochet items, from scarves to blankets.

- **Educational Materials for Kids** - $2 to $15: Worksheets, coloring books, or learning activities.

- **Digital Stickers for Planners** - $1 to $5: Stickers for digital planners, designed for apps like GoodNotes.

- **Social Media Templates** - $10 to $30: Templates for Instagram,

Facebook, or Pinterest posts and stories.

- **E-Books** - $5 to $20: Short guides or books on various topics, from crafts to personal development.

- **Meal Prep and Recipe Guides** - $4 to $12: Guides for meal planning, including recipes and shopping lists.

- **Workout and Fitness Plans** - $8 to $25: Detailed fitness programs targeting different goals.

- **Photography Presets** - $10 to $50: Presets for photo editing software to enhance photos quickly.

- **Budget and Finance Templates** - $3 to $15: Spreadsheets or templates for managing personal finances.

- **Resume and Cover Letter Templates** - $5 to $15: Professional templates for job applications.

- **Wedding Invitation Templates** - $10 to $30: Customizable templates for weddings or other events.

- **Language Learning Resources** - $5 to $20: Vocabulary lists, grammar guides, or conversation starters.

- **Pet Care Guides** - $3 to $10: Tips and schedules for pet training, feeding, and care.

- **Gardening Planners** - $4 to $12: Guides for planting schedules, garden layouts, and care tips.

- **Craft Tutorials** - $5 to $15: Step-by-step guides for various DIY projects and crafts.

- **Travel Itineraries** - $10 to $25: Detailed guides for popular travel destinations, including tips and schedules.

- **Music Theory Guides** - $5 to $15: Basics of music theory, exercises, and lesson plans.

- **Budgeting Templates for Families** - $6 to $18: Easy-to-use spreadsheets helping families manage finances better.

- **Yoga Pose Illustrations** - $5 to $20: Beautifully designed posters and cards showcasing various yoga poses.

- **Gourmet Coffee Brewing Guide** - $7 to $15: A downloadable booklet sharing secrets to brewing café-quality coffee at home.

- **Beginner's Guide to Home Brewing** - $10 to $25: E-books or video series for crafting beer or wine in the comfort of your kitchen.

- **Landscaping Design Templates** - $15 to $30: Digital blueprints for DIYers looking to beautify their outdoor spaces.

- **Handyman How-To Guides** - $8 to $20: Step-by-step instructions for common home repairs and improvements.

- **Virtual Interior Design Consultation** - $50 to $200: Personalized advice on revamping spaces, delivered digitally.

- **Mindfulness and Meditation Audio Tracks** - $2 to $10: Guided sessions to promote relaxation and mental clarity.

- **DIY Natural Beauty Recipes** - $5 to $15: Guides for creating homemade skincare products using natural ingredients.

- **Photography Composition Course** - $20 to $100: Comprehensive tutorials on capturing stunning photographs.

- **Sustainable Living Starter Kit** - $10 to $30: Tips and tricks for reducing waste and living a more eco-friendly lifestyle.

- **Personal Branding PDF** - $15 to $35: Strategies for building a powerful personal brand online.

- **Freelance Success Blueprint** - $25 to $75: A course on turning freelance gigs into a thriving business.

- **Expert Podcasting Kit** - $30 to $90: A guide covering everything from starting a podcast to monetizing it.

- **Email Marketing Templates** - $10 to $30: Ready-to-use templates designed to boost open rates and conversions.

And that's a wrap on our whirlwind tour of digital asset ideas! This isn't just a list; it's a nudge to get you thinking about how you can play in the digital sandbox. Whether something from the list sparked an idea or got you thinking about your own unique twist, the next step is all yours. The digital world is vast and always on the lookout for fresh content and new creators. With a bit of creativity and some action, you're more than ready to join in and start making something that matters to you and, potentially, to a whole bunch of other people too. Let's get cracking!

# Finding Your Niche

Navigating the vast digital landscape to find your niche is akin to embarking on a treasure hunt. The map? Your interests, passions, and the gaps in the market. The treasure? A niche that not only excites you but also offers a potential audience eager for your content. This chapter is about charting your course through this exploration, pinpointing a niche that feels less like a strategic choice and more like a calling.

First, let's debunk a common myth: that your niche must be something so unique, so unheard of, that you're the sole flag-bearer. In reality, the essence of finding your niche lies not in discovering an uncharted territory but in adding your unique voice to a chorus, in a way that makes people stop and listen.

Imagine you're at a bustling market. There are countless stalls, each offering something different, yet some have crowds gathered around them. Why? It's not always because they're selling something no one else is, but because they're presenting it in a way that resonates with their audience. They've found their niche not in the product but in the presentation, the personal touch, the story they tell. Your digital asset, your niche, should do the same.

Start by listing your passions and interests. No filter, just let it all out. Love baking? Write it down. Fascinated by the stars? Add it. Can't get enough of DIY home projects? That goes on the list too. Then, take a step further. What within those interests truly captivates you? Is it the science behind the perfect sourdough bread? The tales of constellations? The transformation of spaces with simple hacks? This is you, starting to narrow down your focus.

Now, look outward. What are people searching for? What questions are they asking online that your passion or interest can answer? Tools like Google Trends, forums like Reddit, or platforms like Quora can offer insights into the minds of potential audiences. But remember, the goal isn't to chase trends blindly but to find where your interests and the market's needs intersect.

This intersection is where your niche awaits, but it's not enough to simply identify it. You must also evaluate its viability. Ask yourself, is there an audience willing to engage with this content? How crowded is this niche, and can I offer something that stands out? Is there potential for monetization? These questions aren't meant to deter you but to ensure that your passion project is grounded in practicality.

As you hone in on your niche, remember, authenticity is your greatest ally. Your niche should feel like a natural extension of yourself, something you can talk about or work on tirelessly, not because you have to, but because you want to. It's this authenticity that will attract and retain your audience, transforming them from passive consumers to engaged community members.

In the quest to find your niche, patience is key. It's a process of introspection, market research, and sometimes, trial and error. But when you find it, everything clicks. Your content flows more freely, your audience grows more engaged, and you feel a sense of alignment between your passion and your digital assets.

As we wrap up this chapter, consider your niche as the foundation upon which you'll build your digital asset empire. It's the starting point of a journey that's uniquely yours, a blend of personal passion and market potential. And remember, finding your niche is not the end but the beginning of crafting digital assets that resonate, engage, and, ultimately, succeed.

# The Creation Process

The creation process, at its core, is about turning your spark of an idea into a blazing beacon that lights up the digital world. Now, let's sprinkle a bit of magic dust on it — AI tools. These tools are not just aids; they are your collaborators in the digital creation journey, making the process not just manageable, but excitingly accessible.

Embracing AI in the creation process is like having a superpower. Think about it. Staring at a blank page? AI writing assistants can help you break through writer's block by generating ideas or even entire paragraphs that you can refine and make your own. Struggling with design? AI-driven design tools can help you create stunning visuals, even if you can't tell the difference between teal and turquoise. These tools are here

to amplify your creativity, not replace
it.

Let's dive deeper into how AI can
transform the creation process. For
writers, tools like Grammarly or
ProWritingAid not only polish your
grammar but also enhance your style,
making your prose more engaging and
readable. And for those looking to
publish eBooks, platforms like
Scrivener organize your chapters and
notes, making the daunting task of
writing a book feel like a walk in the
park.

For course creators, AI doesn't just stop
at content creation. Platforms like
Teachable or Thinkific use AI to
analyze learner data, helping you
understand what works and what
doesn't, ensuring your courses are not
just informative but truly impactful.

And here's the kicker: you don't need to be a tech wizard to use these tools. They're designed for everyone. The user interfaces are intuitive, often just a matter of drag-and-drop or type-and-click. The goal is to let you focus on what you do best — creating — while the AI takes care of the heavy lifting.

Now, if you're thinking, "But I'm not a techie," or "I've never used AI before," let me stop you right there. Every expert was once a beginner. The digital landscape is evolving, and so are the tools at our disposal. Embracing AI in your creation process is not just about keeping up; it's about leveraging these advancements to bring your vision to life with more efficiency and creativity than ever before.

So, as you stand at the precipice of creation, ready to dive into the process of building your digital asset, remember this: AI tools are your allies. They're here to demystify the process, to make the path smoother and the load lighter. With AI, the creation process isn't just for the tech-savvy or the artistically gifted; it's for anyone with an idea and the drive to see it through.

Let this chapter serve as your rallying cry. The creation of your digital asset, powered by AI and fueled by your passion, is not just a possibility; it's within your grasp. With these tools, what once seemed like a mountainous endeavor becomes a series of manageable steps. So, take that first step. Experiment with AI, play with ideas, and watch as your digital asset takes shape, ready to shine in the digital universe.

# The Impact of Digital Assets on Income

Embarking on the creation of digital assets is not just a journey of creativity and passion but also a potential game-changer for your income. This chapter delves into the transformative power of digital assets on your financial landscape. It's about turning your time, your ideas, and your skills into a stream of income that flows even while you're off living life. Imagine waking up to notifications of sales made while you were asleep — that's the potential we're tapping into.

First, let's debunk a myth: that earning from digital assets is an overnight success story waiting to happen. The truth is, it's more of a slow burn, a garden that needs tending. But once it starts to bloom, it can turn into a lush, self-sustaining ecosystem. From eBooks to printables, each asset you create is like planting a seed. Some will take root quickly, others might need a bit more care, but all have the potential to grow.

The beauty of digital assets lies in their scalability. You create once, and it can be sold an infinite number of times, across continents, without any additional cost. Your digital book on gardening tips, your course on mindfulness, your photography presets — all these can reach a global audience, breaking the time-for-money trade-off that defines traditional income streams.

Let's talk numbers for a moment. Imagine your online course sells for $50. Selling to just 20 people a month nets you an extra $1,000 — passively. Scale up, and the numbers start to paint an exciting picture. But the impact extends beyond just numbers. It's about the freedom it grants you — the freedom to invest your time in what truly matters to you, be it further creation, travel, or simply spending more time with loved ones.

Creating digital assets also opens doors to diversified income streams. Your eBook could lead to speaking engagements, your course could open consultancy opportunities, and your photography could be featured in galleries or websites. Each asset becomes a node in a network, each offering its own stream of income, its own opportunities.

But perhaps the most significant impact of digital assets on income is the shift in mindset they foster. You start to see opportunities everywhere, in every hobby, every skill, every bit of knowledge you possess. You begin to understand the value of what you know, what you can do, and you learn to monetize it in ways that align with your passions and your life goals.

This chapter is not just a guide; it's a call to action. It's about seeing the potential in what you create, about understanding the pathways to monetizing your passions, and about taking the steps, however small, towards building a future where your income is as boundless as your creativity.

So, as we journey through the impact of digital assets on income, remember, the goal is not just financial gain — it's about creating a life where your income supports your dreams, not dictates them. It's about crafting a legacy of assets that continue to contribute, to educate, and to inspire, long after you've moved on to your next adventure. Let the creation of digital assets be your gateway to a life of freedom, creativity, and financial well-being.

# Boosting Self-Esteem and Unleashing Creativity

Embarking on the journey of creating digital assets is not just a venture into financial freedom but also a profound exploration into the realms of self-esteem and creativity.

At its core, the act of creation is deeply tied to our sense of identity and self-esteem. Psychologists argue that engaging in creative pursuits provides a unique sense of fulfillment and achievement, fostering a positive self-image. When you create a digital asset — be it a guide, a podcast, or any piece of content — you're essentially putting a piece of yourself out into the world. This act of creation validates your experiences, knowledge, and perspective, reinforcing your value not just to yourself but to the community at large.

Sharing your digital assets extends beyond mere transactions. Each download, purchase, or piece of feedback is a testament to your impact on others. This external validation, while not the sole source of self-esteem, plays a significant role in bolstering your confidence. It's a tangible acknowledgment of your capabilities and contribution, which, in turn, encourages you to push boundaries, explore new territories, and continue creating.

One fascinating aspect of creating digital assets lies in the constraints it imposes — be it the format, the platform, or the audience's needs. Psychology suggests that creativity thrives under constraint. When faced with limitations, our minds work creatively to find solutions, leading to innovative outcomes that might not have emerged in a boundless environment. The process of adapting your knowledge and passion into a structured digital asset forces you to think differently, problem-solve, and innovate, thereby enhancing your creative abilities.

Creating digital assets can also be incredibly therapeutic. It's a process that allows for self-expression, reflection, and even catharsis. Writing an eBook, for example, can help you articulate thoughts and experiences, processing them in ways that contribute to personal growth and understanding. The introspection that comes with creation can lead to greater self-awareness and emotional resilience, key components of a healthy self-esteem.

Lastly, creating digital assets allows you to build a legacy of knowledge and creativity. It's a way of contributing to a body of work that reflects your passions, insights, and experiences. This contribution to the collective knowledge not only boosts your sense of purpose but also solidifies your sense of belonging and significance in the world.

As we explore the intersection of self-esteem, creativity, and the creation of digital assets, remember that this journey is as much about personal development as it is about financial or professional growth. It's about discovering your voice, valuing your contributions, and recognizing the unique impact you can have on the world. So, as you venture into the realm of digital asset creation, embrace the opportunities for self-discovery, creative expression, and the profound sense of achievement that comes with it. Let this process not only enrich your wallet but also your soul.

# A Life Transformed by a Robotic Vacuum

So we talked about boosting self-esteem and unleashing creativity? Well, technology's playing a big role in that. It's like having a magic wand that turns your creative whispers into roars. Digital art, music, writing — you name it, there's a tech tool that can help you do it better, faster, and with more joy.

Our lives are a blend of work, play, passion, and chores. Technology, with its clever ways, helps us blur the lines between these, making it possible to pursue our passions with gusto while keeping our professional lives on track. It's about creating a balance that feels just right, where work doesn't feel like a chore and passions get the attention they deserve.

Before the arrival of my robotic vacuum, weekends were a blur of chores. The routine was as predictable as it was exhausting: clean the house, tackle the endless list of errands, and if lucky, squeeze in a few moments of rest before the cycle restarted. It was a life measured by tasks completed, not moments cherished. The joy of weekends, the freedom they were supposed to offer, was lost in the shuffle.

Enter the robotic vacuum, a gift from the universe (or, more accurately, a well-timed online sale). The decision to purchase it was not driven by a desire for the latest tech but by a profound need for change. I yearned for weekends that felt like weekends, where time was spent on activities that replenished the soul, not depleted it.

The impact was immediate and far-reaching. Watching the robotic vacuum dutifully navigate the living room, something shifted within me. It wasn't just about delegating a chore; it was about reclaiming my time, about choosing how I wanted to spend the most finite resource I had. The robotic vacuum, in its quiet efficiency, became a symbol of modern liberation, a tool that freed me from the mundane and allowed me to focus on what truly mattered.

This transformation extended beyond just the physical. It permeated my approach to life, encouraging me to seek other ways technology could serve as a bridge to a more intentional existence. It wasn't long before I found myself automating other aspects of my life, from bill payments to grocery shopping, each step further lightening the load of daily responsibilities.

But the most profound change was in my relationship. Freed from the silent tally of who did what around the house, my partner and I found ourselves rediscovering the joy of spending time together. Our conversations moved beyond the logistical "who, what, when" of household management to the dreams, ideas, and plans that had drawn us together in the first place. The robotic vacuum, in its way, reminded us that relationships thrive on shared moments of joy, not shared lists of chores.

Just as digital assets offer us the freedom to generate income without the constant exchange of time for money, so does the integration of technology, like a robotic vacuum, into our daily chores. It's about more than just automating a task; it's about what we do with the time it frees up. This mirrors the process of creating digital assets, which, once created, continue to serve us, earning income, or simply bringing joy, long after the initial effort has been expended.

In essence, the robotic vacuum symbolizes the broader themes of this book: the intentional use of technology to enhance our lives, the quest for efficiency that respects the value of our time, and the pursuit of creative solutions that free us to live more fully. It's a testament to the idea that transformation can come from where we least expect it, urging us to look for opportunities to reclaim our time and unleash our potential in every corner of our lives.

# Digital Assets: Your Path to Freedom

Let's dive into a reality where your digital assets aren't just creations; they're your ticket to financial freedom and a testament to the smart allocation of your most precious resource: time. Now we're focusing on how building an empire of digital assets is not only a path to financial growth but also a more sensible use of your time compared to the traditional 9-17 grind.

Consider the typical 9-17 job, where your income is directly tied to the hours you work. It's a finite system, limited by the number of hours in a day. Now, contrast that with the creation of digital assets. Here, the time you invest upfront in creating something — be it an podcast, an subscription service, or a manual — translates into an asset that works for you round the clock, across the globe, without a cap on its earning potential.

This isn't about choosing the easy path; it's about choosing the smart path. It's recognizing that investing time in creating digital assets can lead to exponential financial growth, far beyond what's possible in a traditional job setup. Each asset becomes a piece in your financial empire, continuously generating income while you sleep, explore new passions, or work on your next big idea.

The concept of building an empire of digital assets might sound daunting, but it's essentially about leveraging your knowledge, passions, and experiences in a way that maximizes the return on your time. Start with one asset, learn from the process, and then expand, diversifying your portfolio. Over time, your digital empire grows, each asset contributing to your financial freedom.

The beauty of this approach is its scalability. Unlike a 9-17 job, where your income growth is often slow and linear, the digital asset realm allows for exponential growth. You're not limited by geography, time zones, or even language barriers. Your assets have the potential to reach anyone, anywhere, multiplying your impact and income.

Financial freedom through digital assets is about more than just accumulating wealth. It's about reclaiming your time, giving you the freedom to choose how, when, and where you work. It's about breaking free from the time-for-money trap and embracing a model where your efforts continue to pay dividends long into the future.

This shift doesn't just affect your bank balance; it transforms your lifestyle. It opens up opportunities for travel, for pursuing hobbies, for spending time with loved ones — all because you chose to invest your time wisely, creating assets that serve you indefinitely.

Think of your digital assets as a time machine, a vehicle that takes the hours you invest today and turns them into a future where your time is your own, not dictated by a job or a boss. It's a future where your financial growth is only limited by your creativity, ambition, and willingness to explore the potential of the digital world.

In wrapping up this chapter, let's not just dream of financial freedom and a rich, fulfilling life; let's actively build it, one digital asset at a time. Remember, every minute spent creating these

assets is an investment in a future
where your time is not just valuable —
it's invaluable.

# Starting Your Journey

As we crest the hill of our exploration and gaze out at the horizon; Here, we pivot from dreaming to doing, from ideation to action. This chapter isn't just about closing one chapter of your life; it's about opening countless others. Let's embark on turning the pages of this book into the steps on your path forward.

**Forge Your Path with Purpose**
The journey ahead is yours to shape. Consider this moment your personal drafting table. Sketch out not just goals, but the paths that might lead you there. Each step should be intentional, chosen because it resonates with who you are and who you aspire to become.

**Nurture Your Creative Spark**
Creativity isn't just for artists; it's the lifeblood of innovation in any field.

Feed your creativity daily. Keep a journal, not just of tasks, but of ideas, however fleeting. Let it be a garden where your thoughts can grow wild and free.

**Embrace the Art of Experimentation**
The path to creating digital assets is paved with trial and error. Each attempt, each project, is an experiment. Some will soar; others may stumble. Both outcomes are invaluable. They are the stepping stones of your growth, teaching resilience and refining your vision.

**Build Your Tribe**
Surround yourself with like-minded individuals who challenge, inspire, and support you. This tribe isn't just a network; it's a community of mentors, peers, and followers. Together, you'll share victories, navigate setbacks, and,

most importantly, keep each other accountable to your dreams.

## Crafting Your Unique Offering

Delve deep into what makes your perspective unique. Your digital asset should be a reflection of what you alone can offer. What blend of skills, experiences, and insights can you share? How can you package that in a way that's both authentic to you and invaluable to others?

## Leverage Untapped Tools and Technologies

The digital realm is ever-evolving, brimming with tools and technologies that can amplify your efforts. Explore beyond the familiar. Whether it's leveraging AI to streamline content creation or utilizing new platforms to reach untapped audiences, be bold in harnessing technology to serve your vision.

**Sustainable Growth Over Quick Wins**
In your pursuit of creating digital assets, prioritize sustainable growth. It's tempting to chase quick wins, but true success is built over time. Focus on creating value that endures, assets that continue to inspire, educate, and engage long into the future.

**Your Journey's Compass**
As you stand on the brink of action, let your core values be your compass. They will guide your decisions, shape your projects, and ensure that the path you tread is one you can look back on with pride.

**A Closing Note of Inspiration**
Remember, every great journey begins with the courage to take the first step. Your aspirations to create, to share, and to impact the world are noble and needed. The road ahead may be uncharted, but it's ripe with potential.

You possess all the tools, the talent, and the tenacity needed to traverse it.

As this book closes, let it not be an end but a beginning. A beginning of a journey marked by creativity, purpose, and the relentless pursuit of your dreams. Go forth with confidence, for the world awaits what only you can give.

May this be not just the end of a chapter but the dawn of countless stories you're yet to write.